Rookie National Parks™

Grand Teton National Park

by Jodie Shepherd

Content Consultant
National Park Service

Reading Consultant
Jeanne M. Clidas, Ph.D.
Reading Specialist

Children's Press®
An Imprint of Scholastic Inc.

Library of Congress Cataloging-in-Publication Data
Names: Shepherd, Jodie, author.
Title: Grand Teton National Park/by Jodie Shepherd.
Description: New York, NY: Children's Press, an Imprint of Scholastic Inc.,
2018. | Series: Rookie national parks | Includes bibliographical references
and index.
Identifiers: LCCN 2017023145| ISBN 9780531231951 (library binding: alk.
paper) | ISBN 9780531230947 (pbk.: alk. paper)
Subjects: LCSH: Grand Teton National Park (Wyo.)—Juvenile literature.
Classification: LCC F767.T3 S55 2018 | DDC 978.7/55—dc23
LC record available at https://lccn.loc.gov/2017023145

Produced by Spooky Cheetah Press
Design: Judith Christ-Lafond/Ed LoPresti Graphic Design

Published in 2018 by Children's Press, an imprint of Scholastic Inc.

Printed in Heshan, China 62

SCHOLASTIC, CHILDREN'S PRESS, ROOKIE NATIONAL PARKS™, and
associated logos are trademarks and/or registered trademarks of Scholastic Inc.,
557 Broadway, New York, NY 10012.

1 2 3 4 5 6 7 8 9 10 R 27 26 25 24 23 22 21 20 19 18

Photographs ©:cover: Tim Fitzharris/Minden Pictures; back cover: Jim Stamates/NIS/
Minden Pictures; cartoon fox throughout: Bill Mayer; 1-2: PCRex/Shutterstock; 3: Rob
Hammer/Aurora Photos; 4-5: Sean Xu/Shutterstock; 6-7 background: Eleanor Scriven/
robertharding/Newscom; 8-9: Howie Garber/age fotostock; 10 top: Adventure_Photo/
iStockphoto; 10 bottom: Gabe Rogel/Getty Images; 11: Jeff Vanuga/NPL/Minden
Pictures; 12 inset: John Warburton-Lee/AWL Images; 12 background, 13: John
Warburton-Lee/AWL Images; 14: RiverNorthPhotography/iStockphoto; 15: Glenn
Van Der Knijff/Getty Images; 16 inset: Christopher Talbot Frank/Jaynes Gallery/
DanitaDelimont.com/Alamy Images; 16 background, 17: Willard Clay; 18 inset: Mike
Cavaroc/Alamy Images; 18 background, 19: Carol Barrington/Aurora Photos; 20:
George Sanker/Nature Picture Library; 21: Donald M. Jones/age fotostock; 22 inset:
Gerrit Vyn/age fotostock; 22 background, 23: Bill Coster/FLPA/Minden Pictures;
24 bottom inset: John Elk III/Alamy Images; 24 background, 25: Rolf Nussbaumer/
NPL/Minden Pictures; 24 top inset: Education Images/UIG/Getty Images; 26 top
left: Stephen J Krasemann/Getty Images; 26 top center: Tab1962/Dreamstime; 26
top right: kojihirano/iStockphoto; 26 bottom left: LazyFocus/iStockphoto; 26 bottom
center: GlobalP/iStockphoto; 26 bottom right: GlobalP/iStockphoto; 27 top center:
Visuals Unlimited, Inc./Glenn Bartley/Getty Images; 27 top right: MYN/JP Lawrence/
NPL/Minden Pictures; 27 bottom left: Mark Raycroft/age fotostock; 27 bottom
center: jhorrocks/iStockphoto; 27 bottom right: Sumio Harada/Minden Pictures; 27
top left: GlobalP/iStockphoto; 30 top left: John Elk III/Alamy Images; 30 top right:
danikancil/Getty Images; 30 bottom left: Kazakov Maksim/Shutterstock; 30 bottom
right: vkbhat/iStockphoto; 31 top: Michelle Holihan/Shutterstock; 31 bottom: tonda/
Thinkstock; 31 center bottom: Wade Eakle/Getty Images; 31 center top: elmvilla/
iStockphoto; 32: Kirkendall-Spring/Nature Picture Library.

Maps by Jim McMahon.

Table of Contents

I am Ranger Red Fox, your tour guide. Are you ready for an amazing adventure in Grand Teton?

Welcome to Grand Teton National Park!

Grand Teton [**tee**-ton] is in Wyoming and was made a **national park** in 1929. People visit national parks to explore nature.

The Teton Mountains tower over the land. That is how the park got its name.

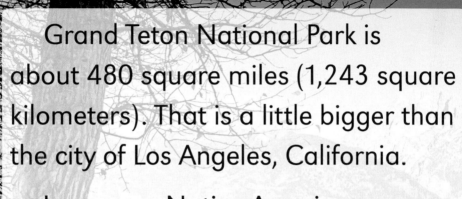

Grand Teton National Park is about 480 square miles (1,243 square kilometers). That is a little bigger than the city of Los Angeles, California.

Long ago, Native Americans lived on the land. The Shoshones [sho-**shoh**-neez] lived in the area when the first explorers arrived.

Menor's Ferry historic area shows where and how settlers lived.

United States

Wyoming

Grand Teton
National Park

N
W E
S

Bill Menor was an
early settler. He designed
a ferry to cross the Snake
River. Visitors can still
ride the ferry today.

Schoolroom Glacier (right) is getting smaller every year.

There are still 11 active glaciers in the park.

Chapter 1

Rocky Mountain Rocks

The Teton Mountains are almost 10 million years old. That sounds really old! But they are still the youngest of all the Rocky Mountains. Earthquakes pushed rocks up from deep inside the Earth. Then **glaciers** helped shape the mountains.

The glaciers moved across the land. They cut deep valleys, or **canyons**, between steep cliffs. Paintbrush

Indian paintbrush is the Wyoming state flower.

Canyon is one of them. It is named for a flower called Indian paintbrush.

Movement inside the Earth also formed Jackson Hole in the park. A "hole" is a flat valley surrounded by mountains.

Skiers flock to Jackson Hole in winter.

The Snake River is the 13th longest river in the United States.

Moose like to eat water plants in the Snake River.

Chapter 2

Water, Water, Everywhere!

The Snake River flows through six different states. About 50 miles (80 km) of it runs through Grand Teton National Park. The river is very important to the plants and animals that live there.

There are more than 100 lakes in the park. Many were formed by glacial **moraines**. Long ago, glaciers carried rock down the mountains. Then the glaciers melted. The broken rock they left behind formed moraines. The moraines trapped the water and created lakes.

Jackson Lake is the biggest lake in the park. It is more than 15 miles (24 km) long.

Some lichens may be the oldest living things on Earth.

Quaking aspen are common in Grand Teton. Their leaves tremble, or quake, in the breeze. That is how the tree got its name.

Chapter 3

Grand and Growing

It is cold and windy on Grand Teton's mountaintops. Trees cannot live there. But moss and lichens can. Some flowers also grow in these high places.

Many types of trees grow lower down on the mountains. They also live along rivers and lakes.

Winters in Grand Teton are long and hard. And summers are short. Only the strongest plants can live there. Sagebrush is one of these tough plants. It can grow in rocky soil. And it does not need a lot of water to live.

More than 100 other grasses and wildflowers grow in the park, too.

Bears often look for food in the sagebrush.

The trumpeter swan has a wingspan of over 7 feet (2 meters).

Chapter 4

Amazing Animals

River otters, beavers, blue herons, bald eagles, and many other animals live in or near the water. So does the trumpeter swan. It is the largest waterbird in North America. The calliope [kuh-**lie**-eh-pee] hummingbird is the smallest bird in North America. It lives in the park, too.

The calliope weighs just a bit more than a penny!

Many creatures live in the sagebrush plains. Male sage grouse spread their feathers and make loud popping sounds to find mates.

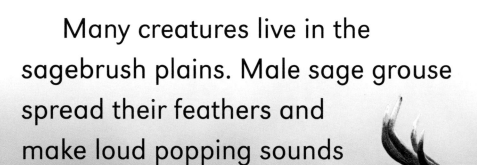

Yellow sacs on the male sage grouse's chest fill with air. They go POP! as the air empties.

Bull elk are noisy, too. They bugle and whistle to attract mates. A bull elk's antlers can weigh as much as a small child!

Elk shed their antlers every year. If you are lucky, you may find some on the ground!

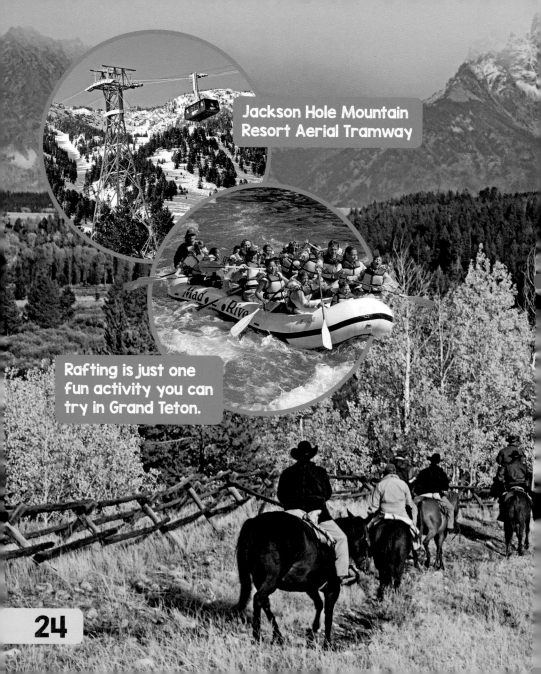

Jackson Hole Mountain Resort Aerial Tramway

Rafting is just one fun activity you can try in Grand Teton.

Millions of people visit Grand Teton National Park every year. They explore the park on foot, in rafts, and on horseback. The park can even be viewed from a nearby sky tram. There are so many ways to enjoy the beauty all around!

Imagine you could visit Grand Teton. What would you do there?

These are just some of the incredible animals that make their home in Grand Teton.

pronghorn

cutthroat trout

sandhill crane

gray wolf

great horned owl

bison

Wildlife by the Numbers
The park is home to about...

300 types of birds   **61** types of mammals

More than 10,000 different kinds of insects live here!

mountain lion

harlequin duck

chorus frog

moose

grizzly bear

pika

10 types of reptiles and amphibians

12 types of fish

Where Is Ranger Red Fox?

Oh no! Ranger Red Fox has lost his way in the park. But you can help. Use the map and the clues below to find him.

1. Ranger Red Fox started with a ride on the aerial tramway. What a view!

2. Next he hiked northeast, stopping at an old pioneer cabin in Menor's Ferry.

3. He continued north and took a dip in Jenny Lake.

4. Finally, he went northeast and hopped in a kayak.

Help! Can you find me?

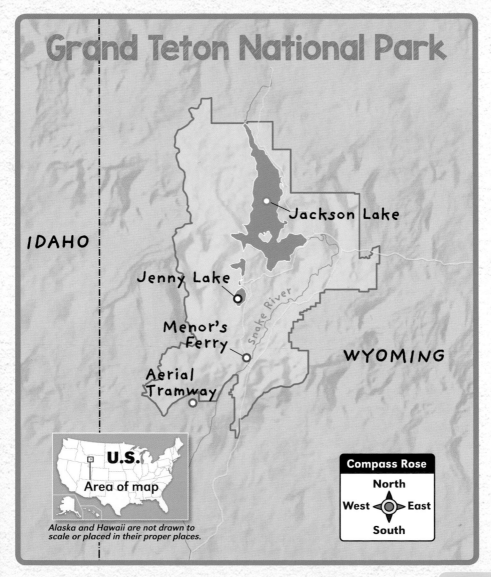

Grand Teton National Park

IDAHO

WYOMING

Jackson Lake

Jenny Lake

Menor's Ferry

Aerial Tramway

Snake River

U.S.

Area of map

Alaska and Hawaii are not drawn to scale or placed in their proper places.

Compass Rose

North

West ◆ East

South

Wildflower Tracker

**Match each Grand Teton wildflower to its name.
Read the clues to help you.**

A.

B.

C.

D.

1. Lupine
Clue: Blue flowers grow on the stalks of this plant, which can grow 3 feet (0.9 meters) tall.

2. Indian paintbrush
Clue: Its bright red blossoms give this plant its nickname, prairie fire.

3. Lewis monkeyflower
Clue: This dark pink flower has small, soft, sticky hairs in its yellow center.

4. Huckleberry
Clue: In summer, these plants are covered in purple berries.

Answers: 1. D; 2. C; 3. A; 4. B

Glossary

canyons (**kan**-yuhns):
deep, narrow river valleys
with steep sides

glaciers (**glay**-shurs):
huge blocks of
slow-moving ice

moraines (muh-**rains**):
earth and stones that are
carried and finally deposited
by glaciers

national park (**nash**-uh-nuhl
pahrk): area where the land
and its animals are protected
by the U.S. government

Index

Facts for Now

Visit this Scholastic Web site for more information
on Grand Teton National Park:

www.factsfornow.scholastic.com

Enter the keywords Grand Teton

About the Author

Jodie Shepherd, who also writes under her real name, Leslie
Kimmelman, is an award-winning author of dozens of fiction and
nonfiction titles for children. She is also a children's book editor.
Leslie spent a week at Grand Teton National Park when she was
12 years old, and she thinks it's time for another visit!